# Bearing *the* Unbearable

## A GUIDED JOURNAL *for* GRIEVING

Joanne Cacciatore

Wisdom

Wisdom Publications
132 Perry Street
New York, NY 10014 USA
wisdomexperience.org

Library of Congress Control Number: 2024930145

ISBN 978-1-61429-899-1

28 27 26 25 24
5  4  3  2  1

Cover design by Jess Morphew. Interior design by Phil Pascuzzo.

Printed on acid-free paper that meets the guidelines for permanence and durability of the Production Guidelines for Book Longevity of the Council on Library Resources.

Printed in Canada

I am so sorry you had to pick up this journal, because it means you are likely grieving for someone you love and miss very deeply. Grief, sometimes, leaves us without words. Yet narrating our feelings, thoughts, and experiences can be so helpful in processing and relating to our inner world. When we are able to express ourselves, privately or in shared spaces, the emotional energy of grief begins to move through us. We learn how to be with this strange thing called grief—a thing we never wanted, in a strange new world—all while facing the loss of a life we loved and once held so dear. When we give our emotions form in the shape of words made from thoughts and feelings, we can deepen our understanding of our own painful experiences of loss and increase our capacity to cope. Most important, we also learn to trust ourselves, which is one of the most important things for us to cultivate as grievers.

You are not alone in your grief. When my own child died in 1994, I felt alone, like the only person on earth who knew the depth and breadth of this type of suffering. I soon discovered that many—far too many—knew the grief I knew. How did I discover that? Because courageous others shared their own stories of loss and love and grief. The only thing harder than losing the one we most love is feeling lonely in the experience. Sharing helps to connect us with others, bridging the chasm of the unknown and bequeathing a sense of belonging, even in sorrow, to a larger community of those who intimately know what extraordinary grief—and extraordinary love—are really like.

This journal is an invitation. A passage. An open heart. Use the prompts throughout for deep contemplation. Write your experiences, feelings, memories of your beloved. Know that, wherever you are, you are not alone in this. We grievers, we rememberers, walk the same road, some ahead and some behind. But we walk together. Let this journal be the invisible thread that weaves together our hearts and souls and minds as we endure one more day—together, never alone. Let this journal be a space in which you remember and grieve and explore. This journal and its prompts for writing and meditating can be used as part of a contemplative practice by yourself, with therapists, in community with family or friends, or with a grief support group. You may wish to read and respond directly to each prompt. Or read one prior to meditation, and then write down whatever comes forth for you.

Doing this very important expressive grief work is crucial to becoming who you will be in the aftermath of loss. Try not to judge yourself through this. Try, instead, to gently take care of what your heart and mind say, feel, and do as you move through each page, whether prewritten or filled with something you put there yourself. You can stretch into expressing yourself slowly, slowly, as you build the emotional muscle to explore all the aspects of your own grief.

If you're in therapy or a group setting, when someone else shares their own experience, that may be an invitation to engage with your grief journal as a means to understand theirs—and to engage fierce compassion for the other person now sharing their own stories of loss.

You can choose a page in your journal randomly, or make a plan to work with each entry. You can write about the emotional, bodily, social, cognitive, interpersonal, identity, spiritual, and existential aspects of grief. There is no right or wrong way to do this work. This is your path, and it's OK to be, as I often say, the "expert of your own grief."

However you use this journal, please take the time to feel and express deeply—with a spirit of love and compassion for all beings, including yourself.

—Dr. Jo

**W**e will not
cease *to* exist
if we *grieve*
our truth.

**W**e will cease
*to* exist *if* we
*don't.*

Share one of your most
beautiful memories of your
beloved one.

If you could say one more
thing to your beloved one,
what would you say?

Dear Grief,

I'd really like you to know

that _____.

What do you want
people to know about your
beloved one?

*Listen deeply*

and you will recognize other citizens *of the* country of sorrow.

There are many and they are

*beautiful.*

What time of day does grief
impact you most?
How might you make space
for grief then?

If your loss were a book,

what would the title

and subtitle be?

What do you imagine your
beloved one would say to you
in this very moment?

In this moment,
where do you notice grief
in your body?

In what physical spaces do
you feel closest to your beloved,
and what do you feel?

Like love, *grief* can't be constrained by *time* and *space*.

In what ways does your spiritual understanding impact your relationship with grief and your beloved one who died?

Describe a moment, however brief, when you've felt compassion amid your grief from a person or animal.

In what ways has your
mind changed since your
beloved one's death?

Name one thing you believe
today that you didn't believe
before your beloved one died.

Imagine grief as a friend who
also misses your loved one.
What would you say to grief?
What would grief say to you?

"I am here," grief says.

"Be careful with me.

Stop. Pause. Stay with me."

Where do you hold grief
in your body, and how does
it affect you?

In this moment,
what do you miss most about
your beloved one?

What is one thing you wish
others really understood
about your loss?

Choices we
make as
*grievers*
merit the
*deference*
of others.

How has your loss impacted
your sense of life purpose or
your place in the world?

Regarding my grief:
My heart tells me

_____

and my mind
tells me

_____.

How, and where, do you make physical space for your beloved one in your life? Or if you don't, then how might you?

When we
*disconnect*
from our
*grief,*
we *disconnect*
from
*ourselves.*

Name five emotions that you commonly feel when grief comes into the foreground.

Share a time when you

felt courageous in grief.

How have any important
relationships in your life
changed since your loss?

What stories about your grief
hold power over your heart?

*Surrendering*
to *grief*
is an act of
necessary
*courage.*

What my grief most wants from

me is _____.

Communicate your grief,

silently, with your body.

What is something someone
could say or do that would
feel like unconditional and
nonjudgmental support?

Don't let
others tell you
*how to*
*grieve*
any more
than you'd allow
others to tell you
*how to love.*

Share the most intense dream
you've had since the death.
If you haven't had such a dream
yet, what type of dream would
you like to have?

In what ways has your
identity changed in the
aftermath of loss?

Imagine your grief was a work of art.

Describe what you see.

What has surprised you,
in positive or negative ways,
about others' reactions to
your grief?

What self-care strategies
work best when you're feeling
intense grief?

When we *love deeply*,
we *mourn deeply*;
extraordinary

*grief*

is an expression of
extraordinary

*love.*

How do you (or how might you) openly reclaim your grief in a way that makes sense to you?

In what ways does your childhood affect the way you come to grief today?

When your beloved one died,
what else did you lose?

Imagine your mind as a calm landscape. Close your eyes and share what you see, hear, and feel as you allow your grief to enter that space.

Suffering endured
becomes *compassion
expressed.*

Grieving becomes
*giving.*

Pain becomes
*wisdom.*

Who or what has been a teacher
or guide to you in your grief,
and in what ways?

What are assumptions that others have made about your loss that have been unhelpful or even hurtful? Have any been helpful?

What aspects of your beloved's physical

presence do you miss the most?

We have earned
this *grief,*
paying for it
with love and
steadfast
*devotion.*

What I need most from
others is _____.
What I need most from
myself is _____.

What song reminds you of the
person you love who died?
Play the song if you are able.

Have you felt any type of
sign or connection with your
beloved one who died? What
might you look for?

*Grief*
is not the *enemy*
and its shadow
will not
*swallow* or
*annihilate*
you.

Write a poem about your
beloved one in three words.

How is your grief different
today than the day your
beloved one died?

Think back on the most painful
day of your grieving life.
What do you wish you had
received from others?

When I look in the mirror

at myself _____.

Imagine your grief as a loved
one who needs care. How
might you nurture or care for
your grief?

The concept
of closure
                does not
apply to
*grief.*

What do you imagine your
ten-years-into-the-future-self
might say to you today?

In what ways do others affect
the way you feel and express
your grief?

Since my beloved one died, I

have become _____.

If you could say one last

thing to your beloved one,

what would you say?

Share something important that you've learned about yourself since your beloved one died.

Grief is the single most *unifying* aspect of the *human experience.*

Every culture
and every religion
knows about
*grief.*

Here are five ways to continue your journey and stay connected with Dr. Jo and her work:

1. Take Dr. Jo's online course, **Bearing the Unbearable,** based on her bestselling book. Visit **wisdomexperience.org** to learn more.

2. Follow Dr. Jo on Youtube (**@DrJo_bitsandpieces**), Instagram (**@grief_doctor**), Facebook (**@drjoannec**), or on the Web at **joannecacciatore.com** to learn about her new work and announcements.

3. Visit **selahcarefarm.com** to learn about and support Selah Carefarm, the first in the world for those enduring traumatic grief.

4. Visit **MISSFoundation.org** to learn about and support the MISS Foundation, dedicated to supporting families experiencing the death of a child at any age and from any cause.

5. Check out Dr. Jo's other books, *Bearing the Unbearable* and *Grieving Is Loving*.

# About Wisdom Publications

Wisdom Publications is the leading publisher of classic and contemporary Buddhist books and practical works on mindfulness. To learn more about us or to explore our other books, please visit our website at wisdomexperience.org or contact us at the address below.

Wisdom Publications
132 Perry Street
New York, NY 10014 USA

We are a 501(c)(3) organization, and donations in support of our mission are tax deductible.

Wisdom Publications is affiliated with the Foundation for the Preservation of the Mahayana Tradition (FPMT).